THE GIFT OF THEOLOGY

The Trinitarian Vision of Ann Griffiths and Elizabeth of Dijon

A.M. ALLCHIN

SLG Press
Convent of the Incarnation
Fairacres, Oxford

© SISTERS OF THE LOVE OF GOD 2005

ISBN 0 7283 0164 4
ISSN 0307-1405

First published as *Women of Prayer*, 1992
New edition, revised, 2005

Printed by Will Print, Oxford

Acknowledgement

The cover illustration, 'Pont Dolanog', painted by Edward Pugh (1761-1813) shows the bridge over the River Tanat, not far from the home of Ann Griffiths. It is reproduced from the collection Cambria Depicta, *by kind permission of the National Library of Wales.*

INTRODUCTION

The greater part of this short work (which was first published by the SLG Press in 1992) consists of a comparative study of two women of prayer, Ann Griffiths, who lived in Wales at the beginning of the nineteenth century, and Elizabeth Catez, the Carmelite Sister Elizabeth of the Trinity, who lived in France just a century later. It grew out of a lecture given in the winter of 1987 at the St Theosevia Centre for Christian Spirituality in Canterbury Road, Oxford. It was one of the first lectures given under the auspices of the Centre, at a time before a regular programme of work had begun.

From the outset it was recognized that the Centre, established in memory of Dr Nicolas Zernov and his many years of teaching and presence in the University, had a particular call to promote the dialogue of East and West in Christendom; however it seemed important to emphasize that the intention of the Centre was 'to study and promote Christian Spirituality' taken as a whole, and this certainly involved forwarding as far as possible the dialogue within the Christian West between Rome and the Reformation. Hence a lecture devoted to two outstanding women of prayer who belonged very clearly to those two distinct and sometimes warring traditions had its own importance for the Centre as an early indication of the fully ecumenical intention of its activities.

There was a further reason which made the choice of these two figures particularly appropriate to the work of the Centre. Although neither Elizabeth nor Ann had any kind of systematic theological training both were intensely 'theological' mystics, endowed not only with deep and powerful feeling but also a clear and penetrating mind, women with a strong grasp of the essential structures of Christian doctrine, Trinitarian and Christological. Each manifested in her own life the truth of the saying of Evagrius, 'a theologian is one who prays truly, one who prays truly is a theologian'.

In the rapidly growing interest in the study of spirituality which was already evident in the 1980s, it was commonly recognized that the Orthodox had their own particular contribution to make, not only on account of the richness of the material to be found in the varied strands of Eastern Christian tradition—Greek, Slavonic, Coptic, Syriac, Ethiopian, for instance—but also because it was directly linked with the general Orthodox consensus that theology and spirituality, doctrine and mysticism, are inseparably bound together, necessary to one another. The position set out by Vladimir Lossky in his book, *The Mystical Theology of the Eastern Church,* that there can be no true mysticism which is not theological, no true theology which is not mystical—a position which had been received with a certain amount of incomprehension and puzzlement when the book was first published in English in 1957—was coming to be more widely respected and received, at least in principle.

But I do not think that many of us were aware in 1987 that in the coming years there was to be what one theologian has called 'an explosion of Trinitarian theology', a rapid development remarkable both for the quantity and quality of what it produced. Habits of mind, ways of approach to central questions of Christian faith and understanding which had been widely influential for at least two centuries, seemed suddenly to be challenged and transcended. Twenty years before, the old liberal Protestant conviction that the development of the doctrines of the Trinity and the Incarnation which took place in the first four centuries of the Church's life was a fundamental *mistake,* something which obscured the true message of Jesus and the true nature of his mission, was still strongly maintained by scholars and theologians who commanded much respect in the English theological world. In the fifteen or twenty years which

2

followed, however, the situation seemed to have changed radically. Partly through a renewed recognition of the importance of Karl Barth on one side and a growing recognition of the importance of von Balthasar on the other; partly through the influence of theologians in Germany as different as Wolfhart Pannenberg and Jürgen Moltmann; partly from the impact in this country of writers as varied as Rowan Williams, Colin Gunton and David Ford; there emerged, towards the end of the twentieth century, a kind of consensus on this interaction of theology and spirituality which seems to represent what some have called a generous orthodoxy: a position held within the mainstream of the Christian tradition but in a way which is neither fearful nor defensive—as in the past traditional positions have too often been. In the context of this new movement the centrality of the doctrines of the Trinity and the Incarnation at the heart of the Christian tradition is unquestionable.

This whole development has made it possible from within the Western theological world to take up the position of Vladimir Lossky about the relation of theology and mysticism and to develop it further in dialogue with a variety of current theological and philosophical movements. Thus the importance of figures like Elizabeth and Ann can be seen in a wider and more inclusive context now than would have been possible twenty years ago, a context which decisively points towards 'the integrity of spirituality and theology'.

This formula comes from the subtitle of a remarkable book, *Mystical Theology*, by Mark McIntosh, an Episcopal priest who teaches in a Roman Catholic university in Chicago. In its combination of lucidity and openness, balance and good judgement, it seems to me typical of the work of a new generation of theologians who are drawing together scholars of different Christian traditions and schools of thought into a new kind of collaboration. I refer here to McIntosh's book more particularly because it contains a searching discussion of Elizabeth of the Trinity, which in turn owes much to the earlier study by Hans Urs von Balthasar.[1]

Before we come to look in more detail at the life and teaching of Elizabeth and Ann, it may be useful to look a little further into the position of this movement in contemporary theology and what is involved in its attempt to re-establish 'the integrity of theology and spirituality'. Mark McIntosh affirms:

> Perhaps I might call it a characteristic theological stance: a way of grounding all the doctrines of Christianity in God's plan to draw the whole world to Godself in Christ. It is a way of writing about the depth of revelation that equips the believing community to live into the mystery. The Orthodox theologian Vladimir Lossky proposed the following as an ideal: 'We must live the dogma expressing a revealed truth which appears to us as an unfathomable mystery, in such a fashion that instead of assimilating the mystery to our mode of understanding, we should, on the contrary, look for a profound change, an inner transformation of spirit enabling us to experience it mystically.'
>
> As Lossky goes on to point out, this is not a theology whose only criterion is the evocation of piety. On the contrary, mystical theology is characterized by the very definite plumbline it uses to measure all theological discourse: namely, how well does it safeguard the possibility for all Christians of becoming 'partakers of the divine nature' (II Peter 1:4). The concern of mystical theology 'is always the possibility, the manner, or the means of our union with God'. That does not mean that mystical theology is only interested in, say, theories of prayer; indeed it is likely to regard these as for the most part quite secondary. What is paramount are the central doctrinal truths of Christianity: that there has been a true incarnation in true humanity of the true God, and that the Church can only live as the true body of this incarnate Word by living ever more truthfully into Christ's dying and rising—thus to participate in that self-giving love which is truly the life of the triune God.

4

'All the history of Christian dogma unfolds itself about this mystical centre', and it is this approach to theology that, following Lossky, I would term mystical theology—doctrinal reflection that is constantly alive to its spiritual sources and goals.[2]

Even a first acquaintance with the writing of figures like Elizabeth and Ann will illustrate the significance of such a declaration.

When, later in his book, Mark McIntosh comes to consider in detail the teaching of Elizabeth on the way in which she meets the infinity of God in the experience of prayer and adoration, it is the realization that it is the love of God made present in Christ which is the vital and crucial element in her whole understanding of the mystery:

She speaks of letting herself go into the abyss and yet encountering precisely in the Infinity of God, his intimacy, almost tangibility. For Elizabeth, Christ literally crossed the threshold of finite and Infinite and so opened the way for creatures,[3]

to make that same crossing over and movement of return.

It becomes clear that the real definition of the Infinite is given first and last in a love which knows no limits ... von Balthasar wants above all to avoid any idea of God's otherness or infinity as being somehow shapeless, without form or self-definition. Elizabeth is a Godsend for him because she experiences this infinity *as* infinity precisely in God's capacity to give himself tangibly, intimately, even finitely, in Christ. 'Infinity is, for Elizabeth [von Balthasar writes] 'no abstract idea but a superabundant presence—the presence of Christ, of the Triune God, of the saints, who, through their wonderful love, stir up in us a feeling of what infinity is. The real infinite is love.'[4]

When we come in the second part of the present work to look at the way in which both Ann and Elizabeth speak and sing of this paradoxical presence of the infinite God in the depth of their being, we shall, I think, find in them the shared assurance that 'this infinite God is infinitely present, precisely according to the concrete Christological pattern of superabundant love'.[5]

I have quoted from Mark McIntosh's book at some length because it enables us to place the more detailed examination of the teaching of Elizabeth and Ann which follows, in a larger and more comprehensive context. We see a little more of the situation of these two lovers of God in relation to the Christian tradition as a whole; we discover them together as more explicitly part of a great heritage of prayer and faith and loving reflection than was perhaps apparent before. One of the most remarkable things which has happened in the last fifteen years is that it has become possible, through the new appropriation of the tradition of mystical theology as a whole, to see such figures as Ann and Elizabeth as part of a long historical process, in its depths much less fractured than at first sight it may have seemed to be.

A further development in the last fifteen or twenty years has seen Ann and Elizabeth newly assessed and appreciated. In Rome the process of the beatification of Sister Elizabeth of the Trinity was brought to a conclusion in November 1984. Far from being a mere formality, this was the fulfilment of a long process, the recognition of a privileged moment in the life of the Carmelite Order and of the Church in France which linked together in a new way Elizabeth of the Trinity and Thérèse of the Child Jesus, two great figures in the renewal of Catholicism as a whole and of the contemplative life in the Christian West.

In Wales, where interest in Ann has never failed among her Welsh-speaking compatriots, various things have happened which have brought her life and work more to the attention of English-speaking people not only in Wales but beyond. Here too there has been a measure of official recognition and celebration, at least of a modest kind. The Church in Wales has included the name of Ann Griffiths in its calendar commemorating her on 12 August, the day of her burial. So the action of Rome in solemnly proclaiming and celebrating the memory of Elizabeth has been matched, at least in part, by the Church in which Ann was baptized and nourished in the faith, in which she was married, and by which she was buried.

In addition, a new translation of the whole body of her hymns by the distinguished contemporary hymn writer, Alan Gaunt, has made it possible to sing them in English in quite a new way. No less significant are the translations made by the Archbishop of Canterbury, Dr Rowan Williams, of two of Ann's most characteristic and memorable hymns, one of which is printed in full at the end of the present work. This free but faithful rendering of the original is born of the meeting of two very different but exceptionally gifted minds.

The bi-centenary of Ann's death provides a fitting opportunity to reappraise the theological significance of these two women whose lives of prayer are a moving testimony to that unity in God which transcends all human separation.

A.M. Allchin
Bangor, March 2005.

TWO WORLDS, TWO CENTURIES

A LITTLE OVER two hundred years ago, a woman was born on a small hill farm in mid-Wales whose name, Dolwar Fach is familiar wherever the Welsh language is spoken. Ann Griffiths (1776-1805) is commonly recognized as the finest woman poet in the long and varied literary tradition of Wales. But until recently her work has not been available either in English or in other languages. Naturally enough, the considerable volume of critical work which her poems and letters have evoked has also been almost entirely published in Welsh. At the present time Ann is beginning to become more widely known. This growth of interest in her is itself a small sign of the increasing interest in spirituality which is to be found in all the churches, and also of a new concern to give a more just appreciation of the role of women in the development of the Christian tradition as a whole. For Ann is famous above all for her hymns which, though few in number, show a theological and spiritual penetration of strange intensity.

At such a moment it seems appropriate to make at least a preliminary comparison between Ann and one of the outstanding representatives of the contemplative life in the other great Christian tradition of the West. I have chosen, for reasons which will become clear in the course of this essay, Elizabeth of Dijon, Sister Elizabeth of the Trinity (1880-1906). The one living at the end of the eighteenth century, the other at the end of the nineteenth century, there are many factors at the human level which separate them. When we look more closely into the motive power which shaped their lives, however, we shall find significant and surprising similarities.

To make such a comparison will, I believe, have a distinct value ecumenically. It is not only that the two figures chosen can stand as typical of the two contrasted worlds of Catholicism and Protestantism in the West. It is also that both bring to life in our post-Reformation, post-Enlightenment world something which was characteristic of the prayer and faith of the first Christian centuries. There is a patristic quality about their writings which was certainly not in any way consciously contrived: a union of heart and mind, of thought and feeling which, in a remarkable way, makes present in our world the gift of theology as it was understood by the Fathers of the Church both of East and West.

Ann and Elizabeth were women whose prayer had brought them to a penetrating theological vision which, far from inhibiting the use of the intellect, released in them a remarkable capacity to see and formulate the deepest Christian truths. Both were evidently persons of a deeply contemplative nature who believed themselves called to give their lives wholly to the praise and worship of God. Both died young, and they had the intensity and whole-heartedness of youth. While neither had the advantage of a philosophical or theological education, both in a brief space of time had gone very far in their understanding of the mystery of Christ.

In their day, of course, it would have been considered quite inappropriate for a young woman to be given a formal intellectual training in philosophy or theology. For centuries in Christendom theology—in the sense of a discipline which demands a sustained and systematic use of the mind—had been a study reserved almost wholly for men. That a young woman should write with such authority on these matters would have seemed strange, abnormal, a century ago, in France as well as Wales. Scholars have been fascinated and perplexed in studying the works of Elizabeth and Ann. Where could they have got such knowledge? R.S. Thomas asks in his poem 'Fugue for Ann Griffiths', 'How did she, a daughter of the land, come by her learning?' and he replies in the same poem, 'She is ahead of you on her knees'.[6] What an eminent French theologian of the first part of the twentieth century wrote about Elizabeth could apply just as clearly to her Welsh sister:

> That a girl of twenty-three or twenty-four attained, without special study, such an understanding of the word of God as to expound the mystery of grace with such faultless orthodoxy, can only be explained by a deep affinity of the soul with it. To speak as she did on such subjects the soul must have experienced them directly.[7]

Methodist and Catholic

But let us look for a moment at the very different worlds from which they came. Ann Griffiths was born and lived her whole life on a small farm, in the Berwyn hills of mid-Wales. Her father was a tenant farmer, a man of a certain standing in his own parish. Beyond that narrow world, however, Ann would have been a person of little or no consequence in the society of Regency Britain.

Elizabeth came from a very different social background. Her father, who died when she was a child, had been an army officer. After his death her mother's circumstances were for a time reduced but it is clear that she moved in the best society of Dijon. Elizabeth was educated at the Dijon Conservatoire where she showed great gifts as a pianist, but her literary education seems to have been fairly rudimentary. She had problems with grammar and spelling in French as Ann did in Welsh. Compared with Ann, who had two or three years of schooling in a neighbouring village, Elizabeth was a highly educated young woman. But neither had received the kind of education which would have brought them within sight of a university, had such a thing been in any way thinkable in their time. Neither had had the intellectual training which would have stimulated and guided the almost metaphysical turn of mind both displayed in their writings.

In making such a comparison we are hampered by the great disparity of evidence which exists between them. In the one case there is almost too much evidence, in the other so little. From Elizabeth we have some three hundred and forty letters; from Ann eight. For Elizabeth we have a memoir written immediately after her death, whereas it was not until 1865, sixty years after her death, that the first full memoir of Ann was published. But although we know so little about Ann, what we do know gives a clear and consistent picture of her character. She was a young woman of determination and ability, a natural leader. In her unconverted days she was a great lover of parties and dancing. Her high spirits did not leave her when she became one of the leading Methodists of the district. Ann lived in a rugged upland area. Her circumstances in Wales were not so different from those of the Brontë sisters a generation later in Yorkshire. Like them, she gives the impression of a very independent character.

Elizabeth belonged to an altogether more sophisticated and urban milieu. At first sight she may seem a gentler, softer person. But we do not have to look far to discover in the stories of her childhood and adolescence that she too was a girl of great determination, with a natural capacity to attract and lead others. In terms of character Ann and Elizabeth had a great deal in common. Both were women of strong vitality, intelligence and generosity of spirit. Both were sensitive and easily moved.

They belong, however, to very different centuries and very different nations. France at the beginning of the twentieth century is not so far away from us. The last of those who knew Elizabeth personally died not so long ago. Wales one hundred years earlier is another world, one in which belief in witchcraft and fairies was certainly not dead; in some ways we feel nearer there to the Middle Ages than to the twenty-first century. Still more, of course, they belong to deeply separated Christian traditions. Elizabeth is rooted in the French Catholicism of her time, a Catholicism strong and yet embattled, feeling the pressures of a fierce anti-clericalism. Ann was caught up in the early and formative years of the Calvinistic Methodist movement in North Wales in a time of fervour and growth, when there had been as yet no definitive split between the Methodists and the Church from which they had come. As we shall see there are many consequences which flow from these differences. One which is interesting is the way in which they have been remembered and celebrated in their two traditions. It is fascinating to see how differently the scholars have treated them.

In the case of Elizabeth, her renown has from the beginning been widespread even though she seems always to have been overshadowed by her older contemporary, Thérèse of Lisieux. She belonged to an international religious order and was part of an international church. Her particular gifts were ones which that Church welcomed and honoured. Her writings have been translated into many languages and she is known in many lands. She is particularly well known, for instance, among Catholics in Japan. But it seems that though knowledge of her is widespread, the circles in which she is appreciated have been fairly limited ones. I do not know whether much has been written about her outside the Roman Catholic world. Inside that world much of the work that has been done on her has come from within her own order.

The situation of Ann is precisely the reverse. She is very little known beyond the confines of Welsh-speaking Wales. But in Wales itself, especially during the last fifty years, she has attracted the attention of very many writers—philosophers as well as theologians, literary critics as well as preachers. She has been the subject of an historical novel and at least one play. More significant is the fact that she has been appreciated by Christians of every major tradition in Wales, not least by Roman Catholics. One of them, Dr Saunders Lewis, has written an outstanding essay on the nature of her theological vision. Another, Fr John Ryan, has made an English edition of her hymns.[8] But other commentators on her work have found in it something problematic. How far are her 'mystical' traits compatible with Reformed Christianity?

Neither in her life-time nor since has there been any problem in principle about Elizabeth of the Trinity. The reality of mystical experience is not in question in the Roman Catholic Church. The only question in her case would be about the genuineness of her experience, and about that there has never been much doubt. Ann's situation is quite different. The very possibility of a life of prayer and contemplation was scarcely recognized in the eighteenth century Church of England. William Law at Kingscliffe (1686-1761) was a distinctly isolated figure. John Wesley, who was himself a man of much prayer, was more than a little suspicious of the 'mystical' tendencies in Law's later writings. Ann too at times must have felt very isolated. It is not surprising that her letters contain expressions of her perplexity, indeed anguish, in the face of the vicissitudes of her inner life. She was having to confront trials of an inward nature with very little help and guidance. The inheritance of wisdom and experience which Carmel represented for Elizabeth through the writings of St Teresa and St John of the Cross, for instance, or the way in which the common life of the community provided a vessel in which her own experience could be nurtured and could grow, these were things which were not available in the same way to Ann.

However, we should not underestimate the value of some of the classical works of seventeenth century Puritan spirituality, notable among them Richard Baxter's *The Saints' Everlasting Rest*, which Ann may have read in Welsh translation. Nor should we neglect the importance of the *seiat* in her life, the intimate meeting for the sharing of faith and experience which played such a part in the development of Welsh Methodism. In this connection her close friendship with John Hughes, the young Methodist teacher who at times stayed in the farm house at Dolwar, and with Ruth Evans—the singer of the three—who was Ann's companion in the domestic care and management of the farm, is of particular significance. The hymns are undoubtedly the work of Ann, but all three had contributed to them.

There is something very beautiful in the spiritual bond which linked together the three young people, in their life of prayer and faith. It is through the retentive memory of Ruth that we have received the text of Ann's hymns. In the year after Ann's death it was she who dictated them to John Hughes, who by then had become her husband. But even so, compared with Elizabeth, Ann was in many ways much alone. The contemplative prayer to which she was called was not part of the heritage of Welsh Methodism. Subsequent interpretation and appreciation of her work has sometimes found it difficult to know where to place her.

A further point of comparison calls for our attention. In 1804, less than a year before she died, Ann Thomas married Edward Griffiths, a farmer from Meifod, and so became Mrs Ann Griffiths, the name by which she has always since been known. It did not escape her first biographer, Morris Davies, despite the vehemence of his anti-Roman Catholic convictions, that there was something in the tone of her hymns and letters which suggested that had circumstances been different, she might have found her place within a contemplative monastic community.[9]

But circumstances were not different. The possibility of monastic life would never have presented itself to Ann. If she had known about it at all, it would have been at second hand, as one of the snares and delusions of popery. Ann lived for the whole of her life on a farm; at twenty-eight she committed herself to marriage, dying two weeks after the birth of her first and only child in the following year. Elizabeth entered Carmel at twenty-one, following a call to the monastic way which she had felt powerfully years before. Surely these facts alone make a great gulf between them?

The answer is that the gulf is much less wide than we might have supposed, at least when seen from the side of Elizabeth. One of the truly remarkable things about her life, which a reading of her letters reveals, is the closeness of contact which she maintained with her family and friends, above all with her mother and her sister Marguerite, after she had entered Carmel. The rules of enclosure were, and are, very strict, but the intimacy of relationship between Elizabeth and her family and a whole circle of acquaintances remained unbroken. The majority of her correspondents were lay people, often her contemporaries. In the very last weeks of her life we find her doing her best from within the enclosure, unsuccessfully as it happens, to hasten on a suitable marriage for one of her friends.

What is even more striking is that these contacts with people whose vocation was in the world do not seem to have been felt as in any way a distraction. Did not all Christians share the same call to perfection? Were not all pledged by their baptism to a total following of the way of Christ? Perhaps on account of the vital role played by the epistles of St Paul in the growth of her faith, Elizabeth seems to have had no feeling that those in the world were following a lower or less demanding vocation than hers. Of the two little treatises which she wrote in the August of 1906 shortly before her death, one, *Heaven in Faith*, was written as a parting gift for her sister Marguerite, already a wife and mother with two young children. Elizabeth takes it for granted that they remain absolutely united in their pursuit of the perfect following of Christ. At least on her side there was no feeling that a contemplative vocation was impossible for someone living in the world with the responsibilities of family and growing children. Whether she would have been able to envisage such a possibility for a Protestant living in the world is another question.

THE REALITY OF GOD

We now leave these considerations and come to the central question: what is it that unites these two women from such widely differing backgrounds? It is, of course, their overwhelming sense of the reality of God, of the majesty, the mystery and the beauty of God, and their wholehearted and immediate awareness that that reality demands nothing less than a total response on their part.

Both have an intense longing to realize in the flux of time something of the stability and fixedness of eternity. In her famous prayer to the Trinity Elizabeth asks at the outset that she may be established in God, 'motionless and peaceful as if my soul was already in eternity'.[10] In *Heaven in Faith* she comments on the Johannine command, 'Abide in me, not for some moments, some passing hours, but *abide* in a way which is permanent and habitual'.[11] Two of the best known and loved of Ann's lines make the same prayer, 'O to abide in his love all the days of my life', while her letters abound in expressions of her longing to be constant, fixed in her conformity to the revelation of God's love as she sees it in Christ. Both feel in the depths of their being that the human heart and mind are made for God and can find their fulfilment in him alone. Both wish their lives to become all worship, all adoration of the One whom they perceive to be wholly transcendent and yet at the same time totally present to and within them. Elizabeth writes in her *Last Retreat*:

> Worship, ah, that is a word from heaven! It seems to me that one can define it as the 'ecstasy of love'. Love overwhelmed by the beauty, the power, the immense grandeur of the Object loved.[12]

Ann sings, lost in amazement before the wonder of God's humility revealed in the Incarnation,

> Thanks for ever, and a hundred thousand thanks, thanks while there is breath in me, that there is an object to worship and a theme for a song to last for ever.[13]

They are both of them people of a contemplative temperament who gaze and wonder and are lost in wonder at what they see, even here and now. But both look forward to a time when the partial vision of this present life will become the fulness of vision in the life to come. In 1906 Elizabeth writes to her sister:

> Think my dear, in his light to contemplate the splendour of the divine being, to look into the depths of its mystery, to be merged with the one whom one loves, to sing his glory and love without ceasing, and to become like him because we see him as he is ...[14]

In one of her hymns Ann prays, 'Oh to penetrate into the knowledge of the one true and living God ...'; and in another she looks to penetrating

> into the endless wonders of the salvation wrought on Calvary, to live to see the Invisible who was dead and now is alive—eternal inseparable union and communion with my God![15]

Already here we know in part. There we shall know as we are known.

But at the same time both are women of keen and penetrating intellect, as well as of powerful feeling. They ponder deeply over their experience of God in prayer, and make full use of the paradoxes of the faith to express and illuminate it. Above all they are people who seem to see everything from the Godward side. The depth of the mystery lies not in the fact that we can love God, though that is in itself amazing enough, but in the fact that we are already loved by God, 'objects of the primal love' as Ann puts it. For Ann the true beauty of the order of salvation is to be seen not so much in the fact that it saves lost humanity , as that it gives glory to God. Elizabeth sees it as her vocation to become a 'praise of his glory', using a Pauline phrase which comes to sum up her sense of the meaning of her life. Both are carried out of themselves in wonder and amazement at the splendour of God. Blessed be God that he is God, only and divinely like himself! It is difficult to imagine two more resolutely theocentric characters than the farmer's wife from Dolwar and the Sister in the Carmel at Dijon.

It goes without saying that, in one sense, this awareness of the overwhelming reality of God goes beyond all words and definitions. Only the silence of adoration is appropriate before such splendour. And yet this experience of theirs is never something inchoate and formless. It takes shape in the person of Jesus Christ, the Incarnate Word of God. It finds expression in the words of Scripture which, for both Ann and Elizabeth, speak with a directness which carries them up into a participation in the divine life. There would be much to say about the way in which they use the Bible. It is a subject worthy of much further study. Ann, with her poetic gift, has a masterly way of handling biblical imagery, constantly linking the Old Testament with the New. She sees the Bible as a unity and in a very traditional fashion finds Christ throughout the pages of the Old Testament. In this way of seeing things she was greatly aided by the two great teachers of the Methodist movement in the North Wales of her time, Thomas Charles of Bala and Thomas Jones of Denbigh, both of them remarkable exponents of the Scriptures. Elizabeth, at a time when biblical studies were not very flourishing in French Catholicism, had a particular attraction to the theology of St John but still more to that of St Paul, above all as we find it in the Epistle to the Ephesians. They are both of them utterly biblical mystics and this is one of the things which brings them together across all their differences.

Trinitarian Prayer

But it is not only the Bible that unites them. The older scholars are quite right. Both are passionately and lucidly orthodox in their grasp of Christian doctrine. The classical formularies of Christological and Trinitarian faith, hammered out on the anvil of the experience of the early Church, are apprehended by them not as abstract and remote speculations but as ways into the very life and mystery of God. For both the doctrine of the Trinity speaks of that mystery which absorbs their whole being.

Hans Urs von Balthasar in his study of Elizabeth says, 'Elizabeth always looked on the Trinity as a space, where she entered and was absorbed'.[16] Elizabeth herself wrote to her sister Guite on Trinity Sunday 1902, at a time when she would have been twenty-one and her sister nineteen,

> This feast of the Three is altogether mine, for me there is nothing like it. It was so good in Carmel because it is a feast of silence and adoration; I have never before understood so well the mystery and the whole vocation which is implied in my name.[17]

Four years later, in one of her very last poems written for the Prioress of the community only weeks before her death, she speaks of this entry into the space of the Holy Trinity:

> On a tranquil night, in deep silence
> my boat softly glided onto the immense Ocean.
> All was resting under the vault of the heavens
> and seemed attentive to the great voice of God.
> But suddenly great waves arose
> and the fragile vessel disappeared beneath them.
>
> It was the TRINITY which drew me to itself.
> There I found my centre in the divine abyss.
> I shall no longer be seen on the shore.
> I dive into the Infinite, there is my portion.
> My soul rests in this immensity
> And lives with 'the THREE' as if in eternity.[18]

And here is Ann on the same subject of our entry into the dwelling places of the Three in One. This is a verse which, it is said, she composed as she rode back over the hills from Bala after a Communion Sunday.

> O blessed hour of eternal rest from my labour, in my lot, in the midst of a sea of wonders with never a sight of an end or a shore; abundant freedom of entrance, ever to continue, into the dwelling places of the Three in One, water to swim in, not to be passed through, man as God and God as man.[19]

The 'blessed hour' of which the verse speaks is doubtless, in the deepest sense, the eternity which awaits her beyond this world in the fulness of the joy of the Kingdom. But it is also the anticipation of that Kingdom as Ann has known it in the worship of the Church at Bala. Through the one she has glimpsed the other.

At the top of her poem Elizabeth put these words from the Athanasian Creed: *Immensus Pater, Immensus Filius, Immensus Spiritus Sanctus.* The juxtaposition of the quotation from what is often considered a rather austere dogmatic text with the lines of her poem, is typical of her, as it is also of Ann. The text of the Athanasian Creed would have been known to both of them from its use in worship (at Prime in the Convent Chapel and at Matins on certain days in the parish church at Llanfihangel-yng-Ngwynfa). Both had the kind of intellect which would have been fascinated by its paradoxical affirmations. Both would have found its formulation of the union of God with man in Christ 'not by conversion of the Godhead into flesh but by taking of the manhood into God', an affirmation which would have answered to their own experience.

It is not surprising to find that in her thought about our absorption into the life of the Holy Three, Elizabeth uses the language of deification much more freely and frequently than Ann.

[The Father] bends over us, with all his love, day and night wishing to communicate the divine life to us, to pour it into us, so as to make us deified beings who will radiate him all around.[20]

She can speak of our being transformed into God by the work of the Holy Spirit. Ann does not use this kind of language. It would have been foreign to the Calvinistic tradition in which she had been brought up. But the substance of her affirmation is the same. The last line of the verse which has just been quoted, 'man as God and God as man', carries in Welsh a stronger meaning than is easily conveyed in English. It could also be translated, 'man being God and God being man'. It too is an astonished and astonishing affirmation of the union of the believer with God, a union which for both can in the end only be understood in terms of the union of God with man in Christ.

Already and Not Yet

Undoubtedly here we are touching on a vital point where there is a difference of emphasis between the two. The Carmelite expresses and expounds her belief in the inhabitation of God in us with an exuberance and a liberty which we do not find in Ann. For Elizabeth we already have our heaven here on earth. God dwells in us, we in him. Time is eternity already begun. For Ann on the other hand the *not yet* of faith is often stronger than the *already* of present experience. But it is a difference of emphasis not of fundamental conviction. I cannot agree with a recent commentator in Wales who, having said very perceptive things about Ann as a writer, goes on to say,

If one means by mystical a religion that allows man to have union with God now, then Ann is clearly no mystic. Her desire for the bridegroom is still unfulfilled—as it must be in terms of Protestant theology.[21]

21

This seems to me to make the difference altogether too categorical and to underestimate the sense of what is already given now, which we find in Ann. The union with God in Christ for which Ann longs and to which she looks is a union which she already knows here below, at least in part, despite and through all the frailties of the flesh. It is because she already knows it in part that her longing for its fulfilment is so intense. On the other hand, the union in which Elizabeth rejoices as a present reality is certainly not complete. She is wholly turned in ardent longing towards a consummation which shall be hers only in the world beyond the grave.

Both women are consumed with a passionate desire to enter into that world, 'the great world which lasts forever' as Ann calls it in her letters. Both can look towards death in a perspective which may astonish us. Both are living their lives from eternity to eternity here and now, sure that what matters most is that our being is rooted in eternity and that we are loved with an everlasting love.

We can however see this difference of emphasis between the *already* and the *not yet* in many places where it would be easy enough to make a complete opposition between them. Let us consider the Eucharist for instance. Elizabeth lived by the daily Mass. She had all the teaching of her Church about the presence and the sacrifice of Christ at the very heart of her faith. In particular she had a great devotion to Christ present in the blessed sacrament reserved. The Christ present in the depths of our hearts is also present before us on the altar. In a formulation which is altogether typical of the piety of her time, she speaks of herself in her enclosure as the prisoner of the Prisoner in the Tabernacle. For Ann, Communion was celebrated once a month. Prayer before the reserved sacrament was of course totally unknown to her. The sacrament was nowhere reserved in the Church of England in her day.[22] Ann says nothing directly about the Eucharist in her hymns and very little in her letters. But we should make a great mistake if for this reason we thought that the sacrament was of no importance to her.

We have already seen a verse which is connected with her visits to Bala to the monthly Communion Sundays there. These visits were evidently moments of great importance to her. The journey of more than twenty miles over the Berwyn hills is difficult enough today; it was more difficult then. When they went on foot, the pilgrims set out on Saturday, stopping the night at Llanwddyn on the way, and setting out again very early on the Sunday morning in order to arrive in Bala by eleven o'clock. Again on the return journey, when Ann would go over the points of the sermon with her companions, they must have rested the night at Llanwddyn. What did they find when they got to Bala? Thomas Charles, who was both celebrant and preacher, was the leader of the Methodist movement in North Wales; a priest in the Church of England, he now ministered in his own chapel. Doubtless he would have embellished the Prayer Book rite with hymns and extempore prayers, as well as with his preaching. But at its heart the service would have been the same eucharistic rite with which Ann would have been familiar in her parish church, Archbishop Thomas Cranmer's rite. Paradoxically, through four centuries this rite has nourished and sustained generations of Anglicans in a eucharistic faith more realist and traditional than that of its author.

In the early years of Methodism, in Wales as much as in England, we know that the sacrament was celebrated with great fervour and devotion. There was a Eucharistic practice which was stronger than the teaching which supported it. Even much later a kind of instinctive sacramental realism seems to have drawn the Methodist people to take very seriously the presence of Christ at the feast of his love.[23] Surely Ann, with her absolute faith in the Incarnation, with her vision of the continuing priestly work of Christ in heaven, with her intuitive grasp of the consequences of the

Incarnation, would have rejoiced in the reality of this presence at the Holy Communion. In particular she would have made her own the concluding words of the Prayer of Humble Access in which we pray that we may so eat and drink the flesh and blood of the Lord 'that we may evermore dwell in him and he in us'. Here in the Holy Communion is the heart and centre of the divine indwelling, which if Ann expresses it in a more reserved way than Elizabeth is nonetheless essential for her.

Marian Devotion

We may take another point where at first sight there would seem to be an immense difference between Elizabeth and Ann, devotion to the Blessed Virgin Mary. It is not at all surprising to find that Elizabeth has a special devotion to the Mother of God. She sees her as the model and type of all contemplatives who are called to welcome the presence of God within them, and to find in him their whole existence. In one place she speaks of Mary as,

> a creature whose whole life was so simple, so lost in God that one can say almost nothing about it. *Virgo fidelis*—she is the faithful Virgin, 'she kept all these things in her heart'.[24]

Nothing about Mary is to be found in any of Ann's writings that have come down to us. But we know of an incident which tells us much, particularly since it is one of the rare stories in which we have a picture of her breaking out in public in praise of God. It was on the evening of a day when there had been a gathering for prayer and preaching in the little house at Dolwar and Ann was caught up in a mood of great exultation. Again and again she repeated the opening words of Mary's hymn, 'My soul doth magnify the Lord, and my spirit hath rejoiced in God my saviour' (Luke 1:46-7). The words, familiar to her from childhood by their recitation Sunday by Sunday in church at Evening Prayer and perhaps also in the family prayers which took place each day at home,

24

had entered deeply into her heart and mind. She too found herself identified with the *Virgo fidelis* in her humility, 'she [who] kept all these things in her heart' (Luke 2:51). In such a moment we see a true reflection of that joy, both human and divine, which is the joy of the Magnificat,

> that profession of inspired faith, in which the response to the word of revelation is expressed by the spiritual and poetic elevation of Mary's whole being towards God … the ecstasy of her heart. In her words there shines a ray of the mystery of God, the glory of his unspeakable sanctity, the eternal love, which, as an irrevocable gift, enters the history of human kind.[25]

Time and Death

It is their awareness of this irrevocable gift of the divine love entering the history of humankind which unites Ann and Elizabeth across the things which still divide them. Nowhere does it show itself more powerfully than in their attitude towards time and towards death. In the strength of this love, because it is eternal, we know time itself in a very different way from what is customary to us. In such a perspective time does not simply run down into disintegration and nothingness; rather it is known as a constant passing over into eternity, implying also a constant dying—not into destruction but into life. Death itself is thus seen as a moment of fulfilment, a point of culmination in which life can be gathered up in a final act of offering, an act of love which fulfils all such previous acts, a final Passover in which faith and hope and love are fully present and at work. As Ann writes in her letter to Elizabeth Evans:

> Dear Sister, I see more need than ever to spend my remaining days in giving myself daily and continually, body and soul, into the care of him who is able to keep that which is committed unto him against that day. Not to give myself once, but to live continually giving myself, right up to and in the very moment when I put away this tabernacle. Dear sister, the thought of putting it away is particularly sweet

sometimes. I can say that this is what cheers me more than anything else in these days, not death in itself, but the great gain that is to be got through it. To be able to leave behind every inclination counter to the will of God, to leave behind every capacity to dishonour the law of God, all weakness swallowed up by strength, to become fully conformed to the law which is already on one's heart and to enjoy God's likeness forever.[26]

As Ann sees it, we give ourselves into the care of him who has loved us from all eternity. Our self-giving is in response to his self-giving, and is made in its power. We make our offering only in the strength of his offering, who gave himself freely and totally on our behalf. So too, as she approaches the last weeks of her life on earth, Elizabeth writes as follows to an older friend of hers,

It is said of the Master that 'having loved his own who were in the world, he loved them to the end', and never, it seems, was his heart so overflowing with love as at the final hour when he passed from this world to the Father. It seems to me that something like this is happening to your little Elizabeth. The evening of my life has come, the evening which precedes the day which knows no ending and I feel in the depths of my heart an outpouring of love which is stronger than ever.[27]

So the approach of death is felt as a moment of the heightening of a love in which what is human is penetrated and transformed by what is divine, a love which is therefore stronger than death. Elizabeth writes in another place,

I feel death destroying me, but faith tells me that it is love that destroys me, that gradually consumes me. My joy is immense and I give myself up as a prey to love ... The God of all holiness has glorified himself in this soul, for he has destroyed everything in it to clothe it with himself.[28]

It is very striking that, as death approaches, whereas the Carmelite nun feels herself full of love for her fellow creatures, the farmer's wife with all the cares of her house and family upon her feels herself drawn the more directly into the things of God and is troubled at her failure to respond to the many duties which time lays upon her. It is as if there were a paradoxical and blessed interchange between them. Hear Ann again as she continues with her meditation on 'the way which leads through death', a meditation inspired alike by St Paul and by the Song of Songs.

> Dear sister, I am sometimes absorbed so far into these things that I completely fail to stand in the way of my duty with regard to temporal things, but I look for the time when I may find release and be with Christ, for that is much better, although it is very good here through a lattice, and the Lord sometimes reveals through a glass, darkly, as much of his glory as my weak faculties can bear.[29]

In such lives as these we see something of the capacity of the human heart and mind to know and to love in the face of death itself. They move towards that mystery not with terror or resignation but with an eager welcome, embracing Sister Death as St Francis did, encompassing the abyss of death in a greater and more inclusive reality than itself, giving meaning to that which threatens to destroy all meaning.

Here indeed is a gift of theology, for here we see a capacity for love which is fused together with a capacity to know in an act which involves the whole person, in which what is human is transformed and transmuted by what is divine. It is a gift in which something of eternity has been made present in time, in which the power of death itself is seen to be swallowed up in the creative and redemptive love of God. In people such as Elizabeth and Ann we find ourselves in the presence of human persons who enable us to realize within ourselves dimensions of existence which before we had scarcely begun to imagine. In a time not far from our own we see lives which have been profoundly shaped by the presence and pressure of eternity, by the acknowledged power of the present mystery of God.

It is now more than sixty years since Metropolitan Eulogii in Paris made his great affirmation that 'the walls of separation do not reach up to heaven; men such as St Francis and St Seraphim have already realized in themselves the union of the churches'. But while we have often enough repeated these words, we have hardly begun to reflect on what they imply for the unity and renewal of the churches of God. Nor have we learned to celebrate the mystery to which they refer in our own prayer and worship. There are ecumenical possibilities in the study of spirituality, and in the joint commemoration of the saints given us by God even in our state of separation from one another, which as yet we have hardly begun to explore.

For assuredly what is true of St Francis and St Seraphim is also true, in their measure, of Elizabeth and Ann. By plunging into the very heart of the tradition in which they were raised, traditions widely separated canonically, they found themselves brought together in a large place, nothing less than the dwelling place of the Three in One. For both, the mysteries of the Trinity and the Incarnation passionately received, lucidly understood, became the centre not only of their prayer but of their life. It is true that we can see in the way in which they state their faith differences of emphasis, differences of understanding; they show clearly the marks of the theological traditions to which they belonged. But at the heart of their faith they are at one in their common response to the mystery of the Incarnate Lord and to the revelation of the love of the Triune God. We see in them how the limitations of a particular tradition may be transcended from within by entering into its depths. This is a way of coming to union whose ecumenical implications have still to be explored.

If, as is sometimes said, the twentieth century has been the century of Christian unity, it is difficult to escape the conviction that the twenty-first century will be a time in which the relations of all the major religious traditions of our world will need to develop in quite new ways, in which unforeseen possibilities of mutual understanding may emerge, and apparently irreconcilable differences find resolution in ways we would never have expected.

Meanwhile, as was suggested at the beginning of this essay, we are given in people such as Ann and Elizabeth the realization not only of our unity with fellow Christians of other denominations but also with fellow Christians of other ages. In them we see a relatively recent epiphany of the ancient meaning of the word theology, a gift of vision which, in Ann's words, allows us

> to penetrate into the knowledge of the one true and living God, in such a way as might be death to imaginings of every kind.[30]

In such a way of knowing—which carries us beyond our customary concepts and images—faith and experience, feeling and thinking, are united and in some sense transcended. Our life in time is caught up into a share in the

Kingdom of eternity; our human capacities are raised to participation in the risen life of Christ the Lord. The nature of this vision is powerfully conveyed in the central verse of the greatest of Ann's hymns, a place where theology and praise have become one.

> Soul, look. This is the place where all kings' monarch
> Rested a corpse, the maker of our rest, and in
> His stillness all things always move,
> Within his buried silence.
> Song for the lost, and life; wonder
> For angels' straining eyes, God's flesh.
> They praise together, they adore,
> 'To him', they shout, 'only to him'.[31]

NOTES

[1] *Elizabeth of Dijon: An Interpretation of her Spiritual Mission*, trans. A.V. Littledale, Harvill Press, 1956.

[2] Mark A. McIntosh, *Mystical Theology*, Blackwell, 1998, pp.39-40.

[3] Ibid. p.108.

[4] Ibid. p. 108.

[5] Ibid. p.108-109.

[6] R.S. Thomas, *Welsh Airs*, Bridgend, 1987, p.51.

[7] Cited by von Balthasar, *Elizabeth of Dijon*, London, 1956, p.121.

[8] Saunders Lewis, 'Ann Griffiths: A Literary Survey', in *Homage to Ann Griffiths*, Cardiff, 1976. For the hymns, see *The Hymns of Ann Griffiths*, edited by John Ryan, Caernafon, 1980.

[9] Morris Davies, *Cofiant Ann Griffiths*, 1865.

[10] Elizabeth de la Trinité, *J'ai trouvé Dieu: Oeuvres Complètes*, edited by Conrad de Meester, Paris, 1980, Vol. II, p.125. Cf. *Complete Works*, trans. Sr Aletheia Kane OCD, London, 1984, Vol. I, p.183.

[11] Ibid. I, p.98. Cf. *Complete Works*, Vol. I, p.94.

[12] Ibid. I, p.70. Cf. *Complete Works*, Vol. I, p.150.

[13] A.M. Allchin, *Ann Griffiths, the Furnace and the Fountain*, 2nd edition, Cardiff, 1987, p.30.

[14] De Meester, op. cit. IB, p.357.

[15] Allchin, op. cit. p.30.

[16] von Balthasar, op.cit. p.110.

[17] De Meester, op. cit. IB, p.8.

[18] Ibid., II, p.403.

[19] Allchin, op. cit. p.16.

[20] De Meester, op. cit. IB, p.93.

[21] Tony Conran, *Welsh Verse*, Bridgend, 1986, p.71. The introduction to this anthology of Welsh poetry in translation is a valuable way into an understanding of the Welsh tradition.

[22] But there are examples in the Episcopal Church in Scotland, in the persecution following the 1745 rising, of the sacrament being reserved for the communion of the sick or those unable to attend.

[23] There is the incident of the young woman who was roundly rebuked when she came to receive communion with her gloves on, in the same chapel at Bala at the end of the nineteenth century. Found in R.T. Jenkins, *Edrych yn ol*, London 1968, pp.44-45.

[24] De Meester, op. cit. I, p.121 (*Complete Works*, Vol. I, p.110).

[25] *Redemptoris Mater*, para. 36.

[26] Allchin, op. cit. p.39.

[27] De Meester, op. cit., IB, pp.443-4.

[28] Ibid.

[29] Allchin, op. cit. pp. 39-40.

[30] Ibid. p.37.

[31] Rowan Williams, *Poems*, Perpetua Press, Oxford, 2002, p. 82.

HYMN FOR THE MERCY SEAT

Wonder is what the angels' eyes hold, wonder:
The eyes of faith, too, unbelieving in the strangeness,
Looking on him who makes all being gift,
Whose overflowing holds, sustains,
Who sets what is in shape,
Here in the cradle, swaddled, homeless,
And here adored by the bright eyes of angels,
The great Lord recognised.

Sinai ablaze, the black pall rising,
Through it the horn's pitch, high, intolerable,
And I, I step across the mortal frontier
Into the feast, safe in my Christ from slaughter.
Beyond that boundary all loss is mended,
The wilderness is filled, for he,
Broker between the litigants, stands in the breach,
Offers himself for peace.

Between the butchered thieves, the mercy seat, the healing,
The place for him to test death's costs,
Who powers his very killers' arms,
Drives in the nails that hold him, while he pays
The debt of brands torn from the bonfire,
Dues to his Father's law, the flames of justice
Bright for forgiveness now, administering
Liberty's contract.

Soul, look. This is the place where all kings' monarch
Rested a corpse, the maker of our rest, and in
His stillness all things always move,
Within his buried silence.
Song for the lost, and life; wonder
For angels' straining eyes, God's flesh.
They praise together, they adore,
'To him', they shout, 'only to him'.

And I, while there is breath left to me,
Say, Thanksgiving, with a hundred thousand words,
Thanksgiving: that there is a God to worship,
There is an everlasting matter for my singing;
Who with the worst of us, in what
He shares with me, cried under tempting,
A child and powerless, the boundless
Living true God.

Flesh rots: instead, aflame, along with heaven's singers,
I shall pierce through the veil, into the land
Of infinite astonishment, the land
Of what was done at Calvary;
I shall look on what never can be seen, and still
Shall live, look on the one who died and who still lives
And shall; look in eternal jointure and communion,
Not to be parted.

I shall lift up the name that God
Sets out to be a mercy seat, a healing, and the veils,
And the imaginings and shrouds have gone, because
My soul stands now, his finished likeness,
Admitted now to share his secret, that his blood and hurt
Showed once, now I shall kiss the Son
And never turn away again. And never
Turn away.

From the Welsh of Ann Griffiths

This translation of what is generally recognized as the finest of Ann Griffiths' hymns is the work of Archbishop Rowan Williams. In the Foreword to his *Poems* published in 2002, Dr Williams writes that Ann's hymns are 'still remarkable for their bold and extravagant imagery and sustained emotional density ...' and that he has adopted a 'style of translation designed to be not at all a literal rendering, but an attempt to recreate the progressions of imagery with something of the energy they have in the original ...' He further notes that he has 'taken considerable liberties with [her] verse, so as to present something appropriately fresh (as she deserves).'

FURTHER READING

Ann Griffiths

A.M. Allchin, 'The Place of Ann Griffiths' and 'The Mystery of the
  Incarnation: the *plygain* carols and the work of Ann   Griffiths'
  in *Praise Above All, Discovering the Welsh Tradition* (University of
  Wales Press, 1991).
A.M. Allchin, *Ann Griffiths: The Furnace and the Fountain*
  (University of Wales Press, 2nd ed., 1987).
Homage to Ann Griffiths (Church in Wales Publications, 1976).
  This contains a verse translation of the hymns and a notable
  lecture on Ann by Saunders Lewis, together with an
  introduction by H.A. Hodges.
John Ryan, editor, *The Hymns of Ann Griffiths* (Ty ar y Graig, 1980).
  The text is in Welsh with a translation, and a critical
  introduction.
Alan Gaunt and Alan Luff, trans, *Ann Griffiths: Hymns and   Letters*
  (Stainer & Bell, 1999).

Blessed Elizabeth of the Trinity

H. Urs von Balthasar, *Elizabeth of Dijon, An Interpretation of her
  Spiritual Mission* (Harvill Press, 1956).
M.M. Philipon OP, editor, *Sister Elizabeth of the Trinity, Spiritual
  Writings* (Geoffrey Chapman, 1962).
Mark A. McIntosh, *Mystical Theology*, Blackwell, 1998.

*The following are obtainable from Carmelite Book Service, Carmelite
Priory, Boars Hill, Oxford, OX1 5HB:*

Aletheia Kane, trans., *Elizabeth of the Trinity, Complete Works,* Vol. I,
  General Introduction and Major Spiritual Writings   (ICS
  Publications, 1984).

Conrad de Meester OCD, *Your Presence is my Joy: Life and
  Message of Blessed Elizabeth* (ICS Publications 1991).